GREEN DAD

AN EARTH-FRIENDLY FAMILY HOW TO GUIDE

Teagan Smith

Table of Contents

Chapter 1: Green Dad - part of the green planet

Seeing the title "Green Dad" may seem a little weird at first. It is not something related to the dads skin color. It doesn't even refer to the color of their clothes. Green Dads are one of the greatest needs of the modern civilization. In today's world when the technology has revolutionized the human living patterns, everyone has become least bothered about the livelihood of this planet. Regardless of the need for securing this planet, we have made this earth polluted, insecure and unsure. Green Dads are a step towards securing this planet and exhibiting earth friendly behaviors.

Who are Green Dads?

Green Dads are a symbolic representation of those fathers and dads who are sensitive towards the earth friendly movement. They convert all their behaviors and practices in a way which are least destructive for the earth and its various natural resources. Green Dads as a part of the sensible community of this globe that raise Green Families and Green Babies so that all of them can join hands in securing this planet. Green Dads are the caretakers of the Green Families as they encourage, motivate and raise green babies.

Why this planet need Green Dads?

The Green Dad movement is just a preliminary step

to save this planet. They are needed for the following main reasons:

Earth is a splendid place to live

One may ask why there has been a need for the introduction of this new movement of Green Dad. The reason is our inclination towards destroying the Earth's valuable resources and its space. Not only are our natural resources diminishing but the space over this planet is also in need of serious help. Our daily routines have made a permanent impression on the natural and pollution free environment of this earth. The numbers of commercial areas are increasing day by day while the true forests of the Earth are diminishing at a faster rate. There is an immediate need for replenishment of these natural resources and we are the only ones that can work hard enough to restore the beauty and purity of this planet.

Green daddy means a green guardian

A father is the one who is responsible for a number of responsibilities at home. From raising the children to supporting his spouse a number of different responsibilities are resting with the fathers out there. Another major reality is the role of the father in developing good habits in his children. Green Dad means a green guardian who raises his family and his kids in an earth friendly manner, keeping in mind the need for the individual contribution.

Together we can make the difference
We all are sharing a common responsibility of living on the same planet. We cannot stop from the responsibility of keeping it neat and clean. Moreover, not only is replenishment necessary, but protection from the further damage is also very crucial so that we can have the privilege of owning an intact planet for future generations. Individual contribution may seem small, yet the individual efforts collectively combine to make a difference together. Every Green Dad bringing out his own green children will make this planet a green earth and a safe place to live.

Chapter 2: Charity begins at the home- involve your family

If you are also planning to be a part of the responsible caretakers of this world, you have to pay close attention to all of the day to day habits and chores. Being a dad, it is your responsibility that not only make yourself individually conscious about the safety of the earth, but also induce your family in this venture. This effort can easily make you a Green Dad.

It is possible that your children already know about the green earth but may have not got a chance to make a difference in their everyday life. For these children you can be the motivator. A dad is the one who is the first role model of child's life. So if you are a Green Dad, your children will idealize all the green behaviors. You have to be the role model that shows those around you how to make this planet one that will last forever.

Begin it from your own world- your home

We always talk about the larger perspectives, ignoring the small and practical steps. Such is the case with the issue of our earth becoming polluted and not suitable for humans. Although all of us have been equally responsible for this disaster, we think that our part in this destruction has been so small that we don't need to change any of our behaviors. This is not true. We are sharing this planet, so we need to have a wider approach of extending our efforts so that all of us can join hands together. If every one of us starts involving our families in making this earth green we can easily make our way towards a happier world. If you are a Green Dad you must have your kids on your side with you. Make your babies green babies who are a blessing for this planet. Consider the green earth as a step by step movement in which everyone has to begin the charity at his home and making his small part of this world green and earth friendly. Involve all of your family members in your daily challenge of making this earth safe and secure.

Guide your kids

Being a Green Dad is surely an effective step in making the world favorable for the human civilization. You have the responsibility that before you can extend your efforts towards the other community you have to make your kids an effective part of the green community. Kids need to be guided and supervised. Instead of instructing them all the time, it is much better that you provide them a practical example by showing how to do it yourself. This will be easier if you start involving them in little household chores which can make a positive contribution to a cleaner planet. Teach them why the care of our habitat is crucial and what easy things we can take to revive the beauty of this world. If you see that any of your kids doing something that is harmful to this earth then realize that it is a great time for you to teach them the correct way instead of jumping straight to punishment. Kids are easy to manage if we involve them in what we are doing. Make helping the earth a family activity daily!

Create a superb precedence for your fellow inhabitants

We have been talking about the need for individual measures taken for saving this planet. It is a never ending cycle; you can start your individual steps and encourage those around you to become a part of this movement. It starts with an individual, expands to the family and then to the surrounding communities. All the communities will be gathered to make a green revolution around the globe. So a Green Daddy is actually making his contribution in nurturing an earth friendly family in which his kids are also aware that it is for the betterment of themselves, as well as those of others. When a green family lives in a community or colony, it raises the bar for all others that live around their home. Eventually a number of others will follow the ideal green family, and as a result the whole planet will be a much happier and safer place. This is easier said then done but not impossible. Make yourself a shining example for all others around you, so that you can show that your actions are backing up your words to those that are watching your life.

Make your kids your green force

Guiding your own kids, and raising them in a green way, does not make your responsibility fulfilled. Guide your kids who have contact with their fellows and defend that they need to spread the message of a greener world so that the real aim of the green movement can be fulfilled. Kids are usually a strong advocate of their viewpoint and will stick to what they think is right. Even when the others are not noticing them, they have an innate ability to make them noticeable .So when they will be exhibiting the green attitudes in between others, they can create a strong precedence for their standpoint. A Green Daddy is not alone in his mission of spreading the message of green attitudes as his children will become even stronger advocate of his perspective.

Chapter 3: Green daddy- Setting up your home "green"

Earth is providing us such an exclusive place to live that we cannot thank the nature for such a powerful and resourceful blessing. All the characteristics of earth, as a planet are highly suitable for the human survival. Its vast natural resources, aid the mankind in enhancing the quality of living .The natural resources are a splendid gift, as they are beyond the creation of mankind so they cannot be replenished. The vast reservoirs of water, oxygen and other natural elements are only available on earth, which are the clear signs of the exclusive nature of this planet. All the beautiful creations and various forms of land, including mountains, plateaus and plane land, are only available on this planet.

But the real trauma lies in the carefree attitudes of mankind in securing these natural resources and the environment of the earth. As more and more technology is being added to our lives, it is destroying the natural and the most feasible environment of the earth. The careless use of all the natural resources, most importantly water, has put us at the verge of losing all of it. The enhanced use of automobiles and other fuel consuming appliances have added dangerous levels of carbon dioxide to the atmosphere of the earth which have made the survival human race questionable. Moreover, the vast destruction of the trees and natural green pastures, for establishing commercial areas has further devastated the scenario. All this needs to be addressed as quickly as possible so that the recovery process can be started at an expedited rate. Green dad movement is also a part of this recovery process so that the earth can be made a better place to live.

Make your home best suitable place for a green family. Some of the ideas are below:

Set up the ventilation and lightning systems accurately:

One of the preliminary reasons for the destruction of the natural environment of the earth is the multiplied use of technology in all spheres of life. Whether someone is having some work at home or someone is having some office work, technology has become a necessity in all these types of work. Although we cannot deny the usefulness of the technology and its pivotal role in making our life easier, yet we have to see the aftermaths of its enhanced use. Technology is also being utilized for those simple mattes which can easily be addressed through using the natural resources. The use of technology is bad when it destroys the natural phenomenon.

One such example is the ventilation and lightning systems. We have become so much dependent on the technology, that even the cooling and heating systems of our homes are artificial. We cannot even cherish the natural air, as we live on the artificial heating and cooling systems. Being a green dad you need to modify your ventilation system of your house in a way that the fresh air can easily pass through the house and the use of technology is minimal.

All home accessories must be "green"

Green does not mean that you should paint them green. All the furniture and other accessories being used at home must be made up of natural materials. Moreover the use of different accessories like furniture, carpets, curtains and other accessories must be up to the minimum level. Without the need, avoid getting these accessories. Do not make up your home, a store for the accumulation of unwanted and unnecessary materials. Make sure that the accessories and home appliances you buy are made up of minimum artificial materials. Moreover the appliances you use at your home must be environment friendly and must have a minimum level of electricity consumption. In this way you are changing the habits of your family members and your kids. When there will be less appliances and environment friendly equipments you are contributing towards the safety of this planet. So make your accessories green for your green babies.

Set up a home garden for your kids

The natural beauty of this earth is remarkable.

Unfortunately we have destroyed it so that we can have malls and the suburbs. Being a Green Daddy you need to make your kids admire the beauty of nature. Do not make your house an fortress of brick and mortar. Set up an area within your home and decorate it with plenty of trees and other plants. This green view can entertain you, as well as your kids. Moreover the materials you use for setting up this garden must all be organic and natural. Do not rely on artificial chemicals and fertilizers.

Shop for the green grocery

Your kids will eat whatever you will bring to a home. Whenever you or your spouse goes shopping for groceries, always buy as natural ingredients as you can. Pre-packed food is always full of additives so avoid it as much as you can. Make your children enjoy the strength of fresh fruits and vegetables. Organic vegetables is always healthy. Artificial food processing is always done in large fuel consuming factories. Avoid consuming these products and guide your kids to the pure and natural food. Whenever you buy a grocery item, you have to look for the ingredients which are mentioned on the packaging of the items. Another crucial factor is the packaging materials of all the products you consume. Being a Green Daddy you have a responsibility that you buy those items which are made up of recyclable material.

A Green Daddy is responsible for arranging all the necessary items in the home which are necessary for making this earth a safer and secure place to live. Being a Green Daddy you need to guide your kids and provide them with the examples of the behaviors which can make this earth greener.

Chapter 4: Raising your kids in a green way

Green Earth is a dream of all those sensible inhabitants of this world who want to make it a better place to live. Green Earth needs a lot of green citizens who will join hands to make it a favorable and sustainable place. Many of us may want to bring this dream come true, but when it comes to acting upon the rules of a greener world, we start putting it off as a responsibility of others. All of you, who want to be titled Green Dads, must know that there is a need for maintaining a green family. Raising a green family demands for a number of different living habits which can make us all a better inhabitant of this earth.

Raising our children in an earth friendly way is not only challenging but also demanding. A Green Daddy needs to be highly motivated to raise his children in an earth friendly way. Green dads cannot do it all alone; he needs the support from all of the family members in raising the children. The role of the partner is very crucial in this respect. Both of the partners can strive together to make their family green and a part of effective community of the larger world. A family which is raising green children is actually sensitive towards the responsibility of all the inhabitants who can make small additions in making this world greener and safer. If all of the Green Dads become effective in raising green children they can make a safer earth. The community surrounding the green families can easily get impressed by the activities of Green Dad and his green and earth friendly babies. The only critical factor is the appropriate raising of the children in a green and earth friendly way, from the very start of their lives. Here are some tips for all of those who want to be Green Dads:

The pre-delivery period- it is critical
- Many people think that raising a child means that parents start planning once the baby is born. But this is not the case. Green dad needs to be highly attentive towards the grooming of the baby, even in the pre delivery stage.
- The pre-delivery stage is also equally important. In this stage, you as the father of the baby need to take care of your wife as well as the baby. You have to make sure that this phase of the baby also passes with the utmost care and heed. Take care of the baby in a green way. In this case you need to keep a strict eye upon all the routine activities of your wife.
- The mother's womb is the purest and the most healthy place of a baby. It is free of any outside interruption. Being a green daddy, it is your responsibility to make sure that your wife adopt the green living habits. She should eat and drink healthy and natural food so that the baby can be

nurtured in the best possible way. When the baby will get the natural and pure food from the beginning, he will surely get the awareness about the need for pure and natural food.

o The surroundings of your wife must be earth friendly and green, try to avoid technology and unnecessary use of electrical equipments. The baby must not be exposed to different ultraviolet and magnetic rays. It will ensure that your baby is far away from the harmful effects of this technology. Moreover, by reducing the consumption of this technology based equipments you are actually adding your contribution towards the safety of this planet. These electronic appliances radiate a number of harmful wavelengths to the outer atmosphere of earth, and destroying it with the passage of time.

o All you shop for your wife must be green and natural. It includes all the toiletries and self caring products and medicines. The use of medicines must be avoided until necessary. Instead of taking the food supplements, you should bring natural fruits and vegetables for your wife. Your baby will get all that your wife consumes. So make your green baby nurtured in a natural and earth friendly way.

o All the products you bring in your wife at this stage must be natural and free from any kind of chemicals and artificial additives. The packing material used in the products must be environmentally friendly. The material must not be a continuous threat to the earth, as some of the packaging materials are not biodegradable. So try to consume earth friendly products and facilitate your spouse into doing so.

The delivery phase- get ready to be a green dad

o The next phase after the crucial phase of pregnancy is the time of delivery. It is critical for the health of your spouse as well as your baby.

o Being a green dad you need to choose the hospital for your baby's birth very consciously. The hospital must have a system of effective disposal of all the garbage. It must have efficient standards of disposing the biomedical waste and cleanliness. By choosing an earth friendly hospital you are playing your part in making this world safer and secure.

o Once the baby is born take care of your newborn and your spouse in a greener way. Arrange for a medical room which is having a proper way for fresh air and sunlight. Avoid unnecessary use of cooling and heating systems, so that the environment of the earth can be saved from unnecessary heating. The excessive use of electric appliances is also a cause of global warming. Remember that a green dad is inclined towards helping this earth in its struggle for the revival of its beauty.

- Bring all the clothing of the mother and the child which is made up of natural material. It will help your baby feel everything natural around him. All the baby care products must be natural and friendly, so that the baby is exposed to lesser levels of artificial materials. During the initial few months your baby will be relying on the milk and probably beast feeding only, so make sure that your wife gets natural food in larger amount.

Daddy! Let's go home!! Be a green dad

- Bringing your baby home and cherishing the little laughter is no less than a blessing. But at this stage remember that your green daddy ambition must not get lowered. You have to make all the necessary arrangements that when your baby gets home, he is all surrounded by earth friendly and green arrangements.
- The baby room is one of the most crucial and the most important part of your house. It is a place where your baby will spend most of his time. So his room must be a perfect arrangement of the earth friendly area. The curtains, furniture and all other baby accessories must be made up of natural materials. Avoid the use of air fresheners and other scented products as they are full of chemicals and artificial materials. So all the unnecessary use of chemicals must be avoided to a maximum level. The most excessively used baby wearable is the diaper.

So search for the diapers which are made up of earth friendly material.

o If you have pets around you, make them part of your green dad movement. If there is a contact between your newborn and your pet, make sure that the pet is in a clean and tidy condition. The pet feed must be done in a natural way. Avoid having processed food for your pet. Make your baby know that a pet is another living creature, sharing our habitat so we are bound to take care of these innocent creatures.

Chapter 5: Grooming your kids for a greener planet

Although the guidance of the parents stays with the children throughout the life, the initial few years are extremely crucial for bringing out an ideal personality of the child. At every phase the child needs care and tenderness so that he can face the harsh realities of this world in a composed way.

Not only is providing the necessities of life for the child an essential duty of the parents, but raising them in a proper way is also a part of parent's responsibilities. A Green Dad is also full of these responsibilities. On one hand, he must provide all the necessary arrangements for green living and on the other hand, he must provide all the necessary guidance to the kids that how they can incorporate a green living routine in their life. Encouraging the children to display a particular kind of behavior is very crucial, as it can motivate them to put their best efforts.

All of you who want to be Green Dads are highly advised that this responsibility of being a green dad is not a one time story, it needs continuous efforts.

Discuss it frequently

One of the major reasons for the difference that exists in the philosophy of the parents and the kids is the communication gap between the two. Whatever you want to convey to your kids, discuss it frequently with them so that you can come to know that what the views of children are. Teach them that the earth is precious for us and they should work hard for its survival.

Arrange small activities for your kids

Nothing is more effective than a practical experience. Arrange for small activities in which your kid gets a chance to participate. It may include having plants in your gardens or cleaning your street or anything like this. It will create a sense of responsibility in your kid. Say him to give you ideas that how we can keep our earth clean and free from the hazardous effects of modern civilization.

Encourage him to spread the message of the green world

The most effective part of your grooming as a Green Dad comes when you have kids who have a thorough understanding that why they care for this planet is necessary. You need to spend lots of efforts in making them learn this. One of these efforts include their grooming as an advocate of their viewpoint and helping others learn that the earth is our joint responsibility and we can save its beauty and its natural resources by working together. When your kid will be able to convey this message to other members of the community, you will feel a sense of accomplishment. Train them in a way that they are able to convey and spread this message of earth friendly behaviors. Your green baby can be the source of inspiration for a number of people around.

Becoming a Green Dad is not hard, but it needs a sense of responsibility. It demands that you have an innate passion for saving your planet. A Green Dad is the perfect role model for his children. Realize that we all can work together to make a difference for the planet.